VLADIMIR PUTIN: LIFE COACH

Also by Rob Sears

The Beautiful Poetry of Donald Trump

VLADIMIR PUTIN: LIFE COACH

by Rob Sears

CANONGATE

First published in Great Britain, the USA and Canada in 2018
by Canongate Books Ltd, 14 High Street, Edinburgh EH1 1TE

Distributed in the USA by Publishers Group West and in Canada by
Publishers Group Canada

canongate.co.uk

6

British Library Cataloguing-in-Publication Data
A catalogue record for this book is available on
request from the British Library

ISBN 978 1 78689 469 4

Typeset in Archer by Palimpsest Book Production Ltd,
Falkirk, Stirlingshire

Printed and bound in Great Britain by Clays Ltd, Elcograf S.p.A.

CONTENTS

FOREWORD

A WORD OF WARNING

We had to think long and hard before deciding to unleash *Vladimir Putin: Life Coach* on the world.

The potential risks are great. Imagine a world full of mini-Vlads, pumped up on tips and tactics learned from this book. Your workmates. Your grandma. The smiley woman who checks your card at the gym. All plotting to establish dominion over you and each other, and increase control of their little corner of the planet.

It's a nightmare scenario that no one would want on their conscience.

On the other hand, most ordinary people are surely too feckless, hapless and aimless to go full Putin. The likes of us can't plan twenty minutes ahead, let alone contemplate developing homebrew Novichok in the fridge.[1] Couldn't we benefit from just a soupçon of the Russian leader's strategic mindset and leadership ability, without becoming a threat to our communities?

In the end, rather than simply publish and be damned, we have decided to pass the dilemma onto you, the reader.

If you believe you (or the person you're buying this book for) might be a proto-Putin – perhaps already with a ruthless streak or habit of stirring up nationalist fervour in your cat – we ask you to put this book down now. The dangers of empowering your inner Vlad any further are just too great.

But if you're a harmless goose who lacks any of the wiliness and willpower of the Russian leader, it should be safe for you to read on. In fact, Putin's example might be just what you need to help you get your act together, stop others from taking advantage of you, and pursue some long-term goals for once in your life.

And if you're still unsure whether it's safe to proceed, the following short quiz may help you decide.

How Putin are you?

Q1. What's your favourite game?
A. Checkers
B. Chess
C. Five-dimensional poker with human beings instead of cards and the fate of nations as table stakes

Q2. Do you rent or own your home?
A. Rent
B. Own
C. I've taken over a bit of someone else's house, but we don't need to talk about that

Q3. A friend tells you a secret. What do you do?
A. Keep it to myself, as I promised them I would

B. Yay, gossip

C. Store the new asset in my dossier of secrets until its usefulness exceeds my friend's

Q4. How do you keep fit?

A. I have a dancercise app on my phone but the ads are really annoying

B. Running

C. My workout partner dresses up as a bear and we wrestle for three hours every day

Q5. Your American friends want to go for pizza but you're in the mood for Chinese. What do you do?

A. The pizza place is fine, I can just have a side salad

B. Agree to eat separately and meet up for drinks later

C. Take out ads on their Facebook feeds showing Hillary Clinton French-kissing a musclebound Satan with the caption 'Pizza is for cucks'

Q6. It's your first day in a new job. Do you:

A. Blend in and avoid drawing any attention to myself

B. Be professional and assertive; they didn't hire me to be a bystander

C. Impress everyone by charging in half dressed, with a crossbow, on a dromedary (or whatever other large mammal is available)

Mostly As: You are zero per cent Putin and can read on without putting the world at risk. You might even become a more dynamic person by following Putin's real-life example.

Mostly Bs: Looks like you're a pretty balanced individual, but you may have a trace of Putin in you. Proceed with caution – and stop straight away if you notice yourself interlacing your fingers and inwardly scheming for more than fifteen minutes per day.

Mostly Cs: You're already a proto-Putin. We can't stop you – perhaps no one can – but for the future of the planet, we implore you to put this book in the recycling bin without reading any further.

Whatever your score, if you decide to read on, please be aware that neither the author nor publisher are able to accept liability for any hacked elections, foreign invasions, democratic backsliding or nuclear stand-offs that may occur as a result of this book.

HOW TO MAKE FRIENDS AND INFLUENCE ELECTIONS

'Zis is a zexy Frenchman calling to see if you want to have ze affair.'

SET LOYALTY TESTS

As a self-described 'specialist in human relations', Putin is always testing his inner circle. He even applied the tactic to his ex-wife Lyudmila.

'Vladimir Vladimirovich has been testing me throughout our life together,' she recalls. 'I've always had the feeling that he's watching me. It was like he was waiting to see if I would make the right decisions, whether I would pass the next test.'[2]

She even came to believe her then-boyfriend had tested her with a handsome, mustard-keen suitor who came out of nowhere pleading for her phone number and a date (something Putin with his KGB resources might easily have organised).

Be More Vlad

To test a work friend's loyalty Putin-style, try inviting her to lunch on a day when you know full well she's arranged to get a salad with the new starter. She should sack them off altogether or at the least invite you along. If not, you've got a traitor on your hands. Change her screensaver at the soonest opportunity so she arrives back at her desk to find the word JUDAS bouncing hauntingly around her screen.

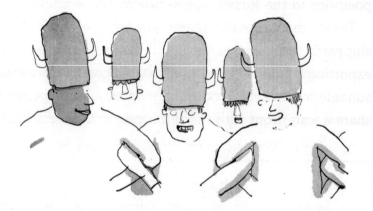

'You're one of us now. There's a secret handshake and you get the
grass verge outside your house trimmed every six weeks.'

FORM A NEIGHBOURHOOD GROUP

The Ozero Cooperative, which sounds a bit like the secret organisation at the heart of a conspiracy thriller, was set up by a group of friends who own dachas on Lake Komsomolskoye, including one V. Putin. After he took power, Ozero members magically rose to assume top positions in the Russian government and economy.

Today these holiday-home owners also own banks, shipyards, gas companies, railways and nuclear fuel exporting businesses. You have to wonder if they are really suitable for their high-powered jobs, or just happened to share a waterfront with the right man at the right time.[3]

Be More Vlad

Starting a neighbourhood group as Putin did could be a great way to meet new friends and make sure local trees are properly maintained. It's also a good opportunity to meet the teenage son from number 63; you know, the one who does model UN, just in case he ever ascends to reign supreme over a large chunk of the world's population and mineral resources.

'I enjoyed our after-work pint the other day so much I had this tattoo done.
It's you and me for ever now, bro.'

START A BROMANCE/WOMANCE

The rapport between Putin and former Italian president Silvio Berlusconi could gladden the heart of the most jaded political observer.

To seal their friendship, Putin bought Berlusconi a four-poster bed, which became famous when Berlusconi allegedly used it to partake of the services of prostitute Patricia D'Addario. In exchange, Berlusconi had a bedspread made for Putin featuring a life-size photographic image of the two leaders palling around, arms around each other's shoulders.[4]

Be More Vlad

Get your friends lavish gifts and you can reasonably hope they'll repay you with all kinds of custom-printed curtains, pelmets, lamp shades, rugs and other soft furnishings, until your bedroom eventually becomes a cosy gallery of your same-sex friendships that none who enter will be able to forget.

'Well, my 12,000 new Bolivian Facebook friends don't think we should break up.'

HIRE A SOCKPUPPET ARMY

Putin's web brigades make him the world's leading online influencer – and you can be just like him.

It's alleged that ninety professional trolls,[5] working from an anonymous-looking office block on Savushkina Street in St Petersburg, were paid by a shadowy organisation called the Internet Research Agency to mess with the 2016 US election. They worked day and night to influence opinion and make American politics seem even more divided than it really was, with each troll typing furiously to meet a quota of at least eighty comments and twenty shares per day across multiple fake social media accounts.[6]

Be More Vlad

Employing your own sockpuppet army on this scale could be expensive, so why not use actual sockpuppets instead? With one on each hand and foot, you can attend your local council's next public meeting in the guise of a crowd of angry constituents, or even as a family of wacky snakes. It's a great way to participate in local debate and advance your agenda just like Putin.

'Before I tell you the total cost, I want you to look deep into my baby blue eyes.'

LOOK THEM RIGHT IN THE EYE

Whatever charm tricks Putin learned at KGB school, they seemed to work on President George W. Bush when they first met at a summit in 2001.

'I looked the man in the eye,' Bush said afterwards. 'I found him very straightforward and trustworthy – I was able to get a sense of his soul.'

Condi Rice later recalled in her book *No Greater Honour*[7] that Bush's reaction had been a mistake: 'We were never able to escape the perception that the president had naïvely trusted Putin and then been betrayed.' (It probably didn't help that Bush started referring to his new friend as Pootie Poot.[8])

Be More Vlad

Eye contact is an easily forgotten basic. If you find yourself dealing with a touchingly naïve individual who's been elevated far above his ability level, earn his trust by first giving him the chance to check you have a set of anatomically sound irises. Propping your eyelids open with a couple of matchsticks can help him get a really good look and confirm that you're not hiding anything suspicious under there.

'And our new school committee member is Victoria with,
it says here, four billion votes.'

DON'T LEAVE VICTORY TO CHANCE

Only one man, Progress party leader Alexei Navalny, is a conceivable rival to Putin in the polls, and he's banned from running.

But even in an undisputed contest, Putin leaves nothing to chance. According to election monitoring organisation Golos, tricks used in the 2018 election included ballot-stuffing, preventing people from entering polling stations and blocking official webcams with balloons and other objects.[9]

In largely Muslim Chechnya, turnout was 37% at polling stations attended by observers, and a hugely impressive but unlikely 99% elsewhere.

Be More Vlad

You can use similar belt-and-braces tactics to make sure of victory at your family's Christmas Scrabble game. Step one is to wait until your aunt the English teacher is too drunk to play. Step two is to replace all your rivals' letters with Es, Is and other one-pointers every time they leave the room. Step three is to give yourself an extra ten points every move for being so clever.

Some might call this cheating. You and Putin know that, as with democracy, it's just how the game is played.

'I won't play you but I'll take on your dog.'

CHOOSE YOUR OPPONENTS WISELY

Putin is so good at quashing domestic rivals there are often none left for him to run against. Not a good look in a young democracy.

In a seeming bid to create the semblance of an open contest, the Kremlin appears to have drafted in minor, sometimes geriatric, opponents.

Alleged examples include Sergey Mironov, whose election campaign included an impassioned plea to vote for Putin, not himself; Andrei Bogdanov, a freemason who is associated with more than thirty new political parties; and Ksenia Sobchak, an old family friend of Putin's rumoured to be his goddaughter.[10]

Be More Vlad

If, like Putin, you hate not winning, pick your opponents with care. Say you're a keen runner in your prime. Don't just enter any run. Find one with an over-90s age category. With a small tweak of your birth certificate and a convincing grey wig, you'll have access to a significantly weaker field of competitors. And trouncing them will be all the sweeter, knowing you were smart enough to all but guarantee your victory.

'My cousin is friends with the brother of the drummer from Coldplay so if you want them to play at your birthday party I'm your man.'

LEVERAGE INTERMEDIARIES

Knowing people who know people lets Putin get secret business done at arm's length. When there was an opportune moment to offer dirt on Hillary Clinton to the Trump campaign, for example, his people apparently got in touch with Uzbek crooner, Emin Agalarov, whose publicist Rob Goldstone happened to know the Trumps.[11]

At the pop star's request, Goldstone orchestrated a meeting at Trump Tower between a mysterious Russian lawyer and members of Trump's shady coterie. Questions as to the level of Kremlin involvement are keeping investigative reporters busy to this day.

Be More Vlad

If you wish to make an illicit approach to someone you really shouldn't, it's time to use your intermediary network. Try asking your dentist's niece's guitar teacher to ask the unavailable person you fancy on a date, maybe through their patent attorney. If they say yes, great, you got what you want. If it's a no, just tell them your intermediaries got their wires crossed and you actually just wanted to borrow a dinner plate.

'Before we start the weekly catch-up, here's a calculator watch for each of you as a little gesture of my appreciation.'

BE MR GENEROUS

If you're a shepherd's son, tending to the flock in the Republic of Tuva, and you wait long enough, you may see only shooting stars. But if you're lucky, Putin will appear out of nowhere, tanned and glittering, and give you the watch off his wrist, as happened to one lucky young farmhand when Putin visited the region in 2009.

He has a track record of handing out highly priced timepieces on a whim to grateful serfs, favouring the venerable Swiss brand Blancpain. He gave another to a millwright during a factory tour, and has thrown others into wet cement at opening ceremonies.[12]

Be More Vlad

If you'd like to demonstrate your largesse in a slightly more cost-effective manner, ask a local street hawker or loitering student if they're interested in a mutually beneficial arrangement. For the price of a sandwich, they'll gratefully accept a donation of a knock-off watch (to be returned later). 'A Rolex Submariner? Thank you, oh charitable stranger,' you can have them loudly exclaim, every single time you pass.

'Guys, leave a few sausages in case Obama comes.'

HOLD A POWER BARBECUE

Putin loves to grill for Russia's industrialists and oligarchs, especially when he has a message to send them.

Soon after he first took the presidency, he brought them all to Stalin's old dacha to serve up shashlik (probably) and let them know what kind of premier he intended to be.[13] Another time, he presided over a BBQ at his retreat in Novo-Ogaryova to advise them not to meddle in politics if they wanted to stay on his good side.[14]

Be More Vlad

Holding your own power barbecue could also be an effective tool if someone is trying to put the moves on your significant other.

Set up your grill at a Significant and Threatening Location. Think graveyards and derelict gas towers. The sight of you in your apron sternly burning your love rival's sausages, and the realisation that you have not invited another soul, should be enough to scare them off for quite some time.

'What a nice photo, it doesn't look like you at all!'

MASTER THE BACKHANDED COMPLIMENT

'He called me a genius,' Trump has claimed on multiple occasions. 'I think when he calls me brilliant, I'll take the compliment, okay?'

Putin's original Russian wording was **'яркий'** or 'yarkii', which can indeed be translated as brilliant. However, it only means brilliant in the sense of bright and colourful, not intelligent.

Putin was essentially calling candidate Trump 'flamboyant' or a 'colourful character'. Another translation might be, 'Oh my god, they're actually going to elect the clown. It worked!'

Be More Vlad

If someone with unwarrantedly high self-esteem lumbers into your workplace, a well-judged backhanded compliment is a great way to cut them down to size. If they have a hide as thick as Trump's they may not even notice, but your colleagues will silently thank you for voicing what they were all thinking.

'If you're worried about getting away safely after the match you can hide in the back of my car.'

SHELTER A WHISTLEBLOWER

Putin is protector of one of the biggest whistleblowers of all time, Edward Snowden, who has taken refuge in Moscow since 2013.

Sheltering the renegade CIA hacker gives Vlad a chance to dust off his halo and repeat his claim that Russia would never allow mass surveillance systems like the ones revealed by Snowden in the US.

'Our agents are controlled by law,' Putin has said, contrasting Russian operatives with American. '[In Russia you] have to get court permission to put an individual under surveillance.'[15]

Be More Vlad

Finding your own whistleblower may be easier than you think. Maybe you have a friend who works at the off-licence and confessed that the special offer Bordeaux was never actually sold at full price. Or a colleague who revealed to everyone that Julie spent more than the maximum £5 on her Secret Santa present last year.

Set up your crate outside the town hall and make a big speech defending these heroes of liberty, and you can enjoy the same feeling of moral righteousness that comes from sheltering a Snowden.

"Fat old daddy", eh? Don't forget we have a baby monitor.'

BE A GOOD LISTENER

Gone are the days when the KGB planted pea-sized listening devices inside walls and suitcases. For one thing, the technology has moved on. For another, a whole range of government agencies are now getting in on the act.

Under Putin's watch, eight different security organisations can access a countrywide system called SORM, similar to that used in the States, to pick up on any phone and internet conversation. Unsurprisingly it's been ruled in breach of the European Convention on Human Rights.

Be More Vlad

Such legal niceties don't really apply to individuals like Putin and you, though, and the fact is, the more you can listen in to colleagues' private conversations, the greater your advantage. Set up camp in a cubicle in the office loos and note down any overheard basin talk.

It may take a few days of eating your packed lunch in less than salubrious surroundings, but eventually you're sure to overhear an incriminating secret that you can use as leverage with HR (for example, if asked to explain why you're never at your desk any more and always hanging around the fifth-floor toilets).

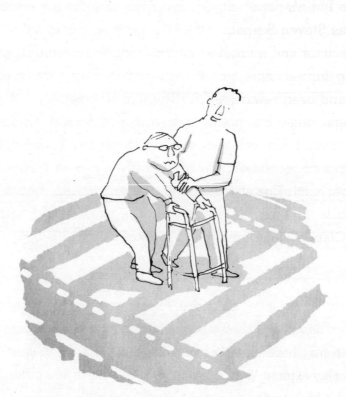

'Can you walk even slower? I want my girlfriend to see me helping you.'

HELP THE AGED

Key to Putin's popularity is his appeal to older Russians, such as Steven Seagal.

The actor and martial arts hero is among a handful of ageing former stars who have pledged their loyalty to Vlad and been rewarded with Russian passports.

Seagal called his citizenship a great honour, to which Putin said he hoped their 'personal relationship will remain and continue'.[16]

Other useful celeb friends he has cultivated include tax exile Gérard Depardieu and big-screen fighters Jean-Claude Van Damme and Mickey Rourke.

Be More Vlad

Putin may have identified a gap in the market that you can also exploit. Why not set up a retirement home for macho film stars nearing the end of their lives? You could dress the nurses as an admiring movie crew to make them feel at home; stage their medical consultations as press junkets; and screen slo-mo explosions on the TVs so they can walk away from them without looking back, just as they used to do in younger, happier days.

YOU TO THE POWER OF PUTIN

'He's calling himself Chief Refuse Officer these days.'

DRESS FOR POWER

You'll never find a picture of Putin looking dishevelled, and that's not just due to the natural survival instincts of press photographers. He knows better than most that power is all about looking the part, using event-appropriate outfits to show he's always prepared and immaculate laundering to project total self-control.

Be More Vlad

Ambitious fashionistas wishing to create a Putinesque power wardrobe should start with a selection of sharp suits (Putin favours Italian fashion house Brioni, but if you do the same, you may only be able to afford the buttons).

From there, invest in at least one of each of the following: a full camo wetsuit in case your pals show up unexpectedly to take you spearfishing; a fur-lined jacket and fur astrakhan hat for touring your local spaceport at the weekends; a sporty black nylon blouson for when the local biker gang makes you an honorary member; a fetching snow-white jumpsuit for piloting your microglider; and army trousers for all those after-hours horse-riding trips (matching top not required).

'My real name's Brian but everyone calls me the Viper.'

GET YOUR OWN CODENAME

At the Red Banner spy school, nobody knew who Vladimir Putin was. Cadets were given codenames in preparation for infiltrating foreign countries, with their true identities kept a secret even from each other. So it was that Putin took the unassuming name of Platov.

It appears Comrade Platov never got to go on a real undercover mission, but just knowing he was becoming a proper spy must have felt pretty thrilling. As a boy, Vlad had dreamed of becoming a real-life Major Belov[17] (a Russian equivalent of James Bond). Decades later, as president, he was also able to impress a bunch of schoolkids by finally revealing his codename at a Q&A.

Be More Vlad

To experience the frisson of a double life for yourself, all you need is the price of a latte. Just go into Starbucks and give your name as Secret Simon, Greg Ulysses (Spy), the Man with the Disobedient Schnauzer, Mark Fake, Yuri Spyalot, or Agent 3,182. Your barista is 90% likely to humour you by writing it on your cup.

'Here's 50p, and here are the deeds to my house.'

TRUST YOUR FINANCES TO A MUSICIAN

You could put your money in the local building society – but wouldn't you rather copy Putin and entrust it to an arcane offshore scheme run by an old musician pal?[18]

Sergei Roldugin is a pro cellist and one of Putin's oldest friends. The pair ran around St Petersburg together and Sergei even acted as Putin's wingman while Vlad got to know that 'cute girl Luda'[19] (the future Mrs Putin).

Roldugin claims he lives a simple musician's life and doesn't have millions. According to the Panama Papers investigation, however, he controls a group of companies that engage in all kinds of baffling seven-figure transactions. Financial experts speculate that the maze-like set-up is intended to conceal Putin's personal fortune, which has been estimated at up to $200 billion.[20]

Be More Vlad

With this amount of cash sloshing around it's easy to see why he'd need a friend with a great big cello case to move it around in. Assuming you're considerably below Putin on the rich list, you may be able to run a similar scheme by befriending a local viola player, or even a morally compromised trianglist.

'This is Professor Anand, the real genius behind
"What I did on my holidays" and "When I grow up I want to be an astronaut".'

HIRE A GHOSTWRITER

You'd have to be pretty smart to write a dissertation titled 'Strategic Planning of the Reproduction of the Mineral Resource Base of a Region under Conditions of the Formation of Market Relations'. But even smarter not to.

It's alleged that Putin's doctoral thesis, obtained at age forty-four from the St Petersburg Mining University, was in fact the work of the university's rector, Vladimir Litvinenko.[21]

Normally Litvinenko charged for this illegal service, but he's said to have written Putin's for free after the rising politician helped him get his job. (It's questionable how good a job he did, as more than sixteen pages of the thesis were taken word for word from an American textbook.[22])

Be More Vlad

If your CV is a bit thin, consider hiring a professional ghostwriter to nab you a postgrad qualification. The thesis they write for you will most likely be sections copied and pasted from other books, linked by stretches of gibberish. But if Putin's case is anything to go by, nobody will bother to actually read it until you've been running the country for years. And by that time you should be just about scandal-proof.

'Sure, I was speeding but what about the brutal treatment of
native American populations in the 1830s?'

PRACTISE WHATABOUTISM

Whataboutism (noun): a brazen move from the heyday of Soviet propaganda, in which criticism is met by changing the subject.

Or as Gary Kasparov puts it in his book, *Winter is Coming*, it is 'a way for Russian bureaucrats to "respond" to criticism of Soviet massacres, forced deportations and gulags with "What about how you Americans treated the Native Americans and slaves?" or something similar.'[23]

Whataboutism has made a comeback in Putin's Russia and is a favourite tool of both Putin's online hordes and the man himself. Challenged in 2004 about the annexation of Crimea, Putin brought up the annexation of Texas in 1845[24] – perhaps not entirely germane.

Be More Vlad

To use whataboutism in your life, keep a mental list of the sins of others so you always have a counter-accusation on hand when accused of wrongdoing. And should anyone challenge you on your rampant whataboutism, just remind them how many slave labourers needlessly died during the construction of the Great Wall of China.

'Can someone help me, I think I've pulled my psoas.'

MANSPREAD

'There's an expression – we certainly know it in New York – called manspreading. Every time I met with him, it would be . . . the whole deal.'[25]

The words of Hillary Clinton, sounding traumatised as she recalls experiencing Putin's body language during official meetings.

Vlad might be a natural manspreader, but it's equally possible it's a learned tactic. Putin took classes, along with other rising politicians in post-Soviet Russia, from 'Mr Body Language', an Australian relationship guru.[26]

Be More Vlad

Mr Body Language would tell you that you don't have to be a man to dominate a space in an unladylike way. Simply visualise a couple of grapefruits between your thighs. Even if you're called out for manspreading by the local Hillaries, they'll know deep in their caveperson hearts that you must be a big beast, whose reproductive parts need airflow and who deserves to rule over the tribe till someone even more bow-legged comes along.

'Table for one, please, and make sure the waiters know it's my birthday.'

GO IT ALONE

As a rule, politicians like to be shown surrounded by an adoring fan club, but Putin is cut from a different cloth.

His 2018 reinauguration included staged coverage of his day as he reviewed papers alone, inspected a military parade alone and strode down red-carpeted corridors alone. Characteristically, he seemed content to have no family to support him, no predecessors to advise him and no allies to succeed him. Even his highest-ranking colleagues were pictured corralled behind a velvet rope.

Be More Vlad

Projecting solitary strength as Putin does is a fine art. Not having any friends is easy; the hard part is never letting on how terribly lonely you are.

No matter how much you yearn to join the office lunch club or latest in-joke, you must stay cool, aloof and above it all. You can always hold your own hand for solace as you weep in bed later. (Something you may need to do more and more as you perfect your self-reliant act.)

'Come in, Jon. I see you've brought round another bottle of your broccoli wine.'

INDULGE IN SOME LIGHT TROLLING

It appears as though Putin likes to blow off steam by trolling the Americans with the help of the Putinka vodka brand.

The award-winning super premium spirit, which plays off Putin's name and popularity, made a genius move in 2014 when it became official sponsor of the US women's bobsled team at the Winter Olympics.[27]

The team said they accepted Putinka's backing due to a lack of domestic funding. But because Putinka is the product of a Russian state-owned distillery, America could arguably be said to have allowed the Kremlin to co-opt a key part of its Olympic effort – definitely a first in the two nations' long sporting rivalry.

Be More Vlad

Trolling your enemies like Putinka couldn't be easier. Just invite them to sample your hideous homemade parsnip liquor, as if it tastes of something other than leftover pickle juice, cat spray, and parsnips.

'That meditation app must really be working,
darling, all your wrinkles have gone!'

FIX THE BAGS UNDER YOUR EYES

Who says there are no new faces in Russian politics?

Following a ten-day vanishing act in 2011, Putin was seen wearing what looked like make-up over a black eye. Was he covering up fresh plastic surgery? Tabloids claimed that before/after photos showed a fuller, tauter face.

The new look suited him well: after all, why would someone who is 100% confident of every decision they've ever made have worry lines?

Be More Vlad

If you'd like to show your mastery over the process of ageing, ask for a Full Putin at your nearest cosmetic clinic. They'll understand you're in a stressful job and want to project statesmanlike calm at all times. Locked in your new Botox bubble, you'll never again betray your panic with a trembling upper lip or eyelid twitch. In fact, from now on you won't be able to change your expression at all.

'MumDadIt'sMeStuartI'mGay!'

USE THE ELEMENT OF SURPRISE

Putin is in a line of leaders dating back to Sun Tzu who use unpredictability and surprise to wrong-foot their opponents (and populaces).

Whether venturing into Ukraine without so much as a press conference, or revealing a military shake-up that his own top brass had no idea was coming, the man sometimes known as the Grey Cardinal holds his cards close until he plays them. By not giving anyone time to take stock, he's able to control the news cycle and leave others spluttering.

Be More Vlad

You can try out this tactic if you want to introduce new company policies that you don't technically speaking have the authority to introduce. Try running stark naked through the office when you're supposed to be away on holiday, yelling through a loudhailer, 'It's nudist Wednesday! Nudist Wednesdays are a thing now!', then sprint out of the office before security can catch you.

Sing out your lines with enough gusto, and the sheer surprise factor may be enough to disorient your colleagues into arriving at work au naturel next Wednesday, and every Wednesday thereafter.

'If you say I'm thin-skinned one more time, so help me god . . .'

SILENCE YOUR CRITICS

Saying what you think in Putin's Russia takes nerve.

Some of his noisiest critics have ended up six feet under, with commentators speculating that Putin ordered the killings[28] (though one man, Donald Trump, insists uncharacteristically on innocent until proven guilty in this case). The dead include Anna Politkovskaya, author of *Putin's Russia* (victim of a $150k hit job in 2006); Natalya Estemirova, who reported on the Chechnyan war (kidnapped, shot and dumped in the woods in 2009); Yuri Shchekochikhin, who wrote about organised crime and corruption (died suddenly of a mysterious illness in 2003); and Boris Nemtsov, who led street rallies against Putin (shot four times in the back in 2015).

Be More Vlad

If anyone says something hurtful about you, why not murder them with words instead? Incredibly sassy and lethal retorts you could try include: 'There's no need to repeat yourself, I ignored you just fine the first time', 'I liked you better before you spoke', or 'Keep rolling your eyes, maybe you'll find a brain back there.'

'Another ten years of this and I thought
I'd have a crack at being UN Secretary General.'

BIDE YOUR TIME

Putin spent much of his career as a relatively junior KGB officer, collecting press clippings in Dresden, far from the real action. Back then nobody would have figured him as a future leader. Nobody had heard of him, in fact.

Yet the collapse of the Soviet Union led to a succession of opportunities in Moscow, and at forty-six he was unexpectedly picked as new director of the FSB.

Be More Vlad

If you feel you're going nowhere and not getting any younger, remember Putin's example and hang on in there. A new historical epoch may be just around the corner and with it a totally new set of opportunities for someone with your particular skill set.

(Let's just hope the post-revolution landscape has special need for an encyclopaedic knowledge of the *Grand Theft Auto* universe, really quite fast two-fingered typing and the ability to tell the colour of M&Ms through taste alone.)

'Well, the pilot will have to turn around then, won't he?'

MAKE OTHERS WORK TO YOUR SCHEDULE

Putin is a night person, which means those who deal with him have to be night people, too. By the time he gets into his office after swimming and working out, it's already afternoon, which means many of his Kremlin meetings aren't even scheduled to start till after midnight.

He has also bent time itself to his will. In 2014 he made a sweeping adjustment to his vast country's eleven time zones, which many interpreted as a pointed reversal of changes made during Medvedev's presidential term.

Be More Vlad

Follow Vlad's example and make others adjust their lives to *your* needs. If your mornings are one big rush, for example, why not feed your kids their breakfast at 1 a.m.? It'll be easier for you and a fun feast for little Jack and Olivia – plus as an added bonus they'll be too tired to misbehave on the school run.

'Maybe if you tidy your room, young lady, I'll turn the central heating back on.'

SHUT OFF THE GAS

Putin has access to a strategic stopcock and isn't afraid to use it.

On New Year's Day 2006, Russia cut off gas to Ukraine during a political dispute, preventing it flowing on to the rest of Europe.

For two weeks, in the middle of a bitingly cold winter, the pressure in pipes even as far away as France fell alarmingly. Eventually, Putin forced Ukraine into a deal and a crisis was averted, but it was interpreted as a sign of how far he'd go to press a point and get his way.

Be More Vlad

If you have kids, or might do some day, you too can block access to essential commodities to get what you want. For example, say no to ice cream till they do the washing-up; turn off the Wi-Fi till they've finished their homework; or withhold love and affection until they become emotionally callused and manipulative adults like their mum and dad.

THE TWELVE TACTICS OF
HIGHLY RUTHLESS PEOPLE

'He wasn't looking at me funny but he looked like he might be about to.'

STRIKE FIRST

As a youth Putin learned to be quick on the attack, carrying a knife at school and brawling in the courtyard of his parents' apartment block.

He once threw a man over his shoulder, just like in the dojo, after he tried to cadge a cigarette.

'If a fight is inevitable, you have to hit first,'[29] he said decades later, explaining his snap decision to loose jets on ISIS forces in Syria.

Acting without warning anyone, even his supposed allies, made it seem as if he was in charge of the global war on terror while everyone else had to scramble to respond.

Be More Vlad

We can all apply this lesson from the mean streets of St Petersburg. Say you see conflict coming in the form of a parking warden heading towards your vehicle. Don't stutter excuses. Slap a handwritten ticket of your own on the warden's hat.

He'll be so thrown by your initiative that you may even be able to drive away with a profit.

'Before we start, has anyone seen my pet tarantula?'

PLAY ON PEOPLE'S PHOBIAS

Putin's been accused of using his pet Labrador to frighten Angela Merkel, after being briefed on her lifelong fear of dogs. The large black Lab, incongruously named Connie Paulgrave, was brought into one of their first meetings to Merkel's visible discomfort.

Putin denies it was a power play, but if it was, it was a good one.

Be More Vlad

Do you want to play on people's fears to gain the upper hand in a deal? No problem: before you haggle over a used car, stick in a pair of Dracula teeth. In common with all rational humans, the salesperson's deep primal terror of Nosferatu, aka Count Orko, the 'bird of death', will likely lead him to accept a lowball offer so he can end the terrifying encounter asap.

'Begone, revenant, back to your Carpathian grave in your bargain Renault Clio,' you'll likely hear him muttering as he hands over the keys.

'I'm deleting you from my contacts, Peter.
I'm serious. I can't handle your negativity.'

CUT OUT TOXIC FRIENDSHIPS

Boris Berezovsky was one of Putin's closest allies. They went on skiing trips and Spanish villa holidays together. It was Boris, a Kremlin insider, who was sent to personally offer Putin the post-Yeltsin presidency.

But soon after Vlad took the job, the friendship soured. Berezovsky wrote an open letter protesting legislation that would allow Putin to dismiss elected governors, saying he could not be part of 'the restoration of an authoritarian regime'.[30] He went on to criticise Putin for his handling of the Kursk submarine tragedy in which 118 sailors died.

Be More Vlad

Putin didn't need this kind of negative energy and judgement in his life and neither do you. Instead of letting your toxic friend drag you down, do as Putin did: forcibly confiscate any companies and TV channels they have, exile them to London and allegedly have them strangled in their bathroom (nothing was ever proven).

Cutting someone out of your life may feel awkward at the time, but you need to make the decision that's best for you and the personal journey you're on.

'FYI I spat in your Caesar salad.'

SERVE REVENGE COLD IN A HIGH STREET RESTAURANT

Putin's FSB intelligence service has a long memory.

Agents who've fled the country seem to find themselves becoming mysteriously ill, sometimes years after their defection, including Alexander Litvinenko (poisoned by radiation in sushi eatery Itsu) and Sergei Skripal (exposed to nerve agent in Italian restaurant Zizzi).

It's supposed that these exotic killing techniques were chosen as a warning to others – to keep their mouths shut, as well as to steer clear of England's mid-priced chain restaurant scene.

Be More Vlad

If a friend lets you down – perhaps by moving away for work and not answering your texts any more – you can take revenge FSB-style by organising a reunion and slipping a fast-acting laxative in their pasta. Call it spaghetti Putinesca.

When they make their excuses to leave, say loudly, so everyone gets your emphasis, 'I'm sorry you need to go.' Your other friends will get the message, especially when you start making fart noises. That is to say, they'll know it was you, but they'll never be able to prove it. In intelligence circles it's called 'implausible deniability'.

'I'm looking into digging a bunker, but in the meantime these pans will do.'

PREPARE FOR ARMAGEDDON

In a world of nuclear-equipped madmen, it's reassuring to know that Putin has been busily prepping for World War Three.

In March 2018 he revealed nuclear attack technologies including 'invincible' warheads with unlimited strike range. A CGI video showed them raining down on what looked like Florida.

'I hope everything that was said today will sober up potential aggressors,'[31] he commented.

Nuclear experts also believe Putin has been strengthening Dead Hand, the system designed to unleash the entire nuclear arsenal at once in the event of a decapitation strike on Moscow.

Be More Vlad

Chances are you'll be a pile of ash if a nuclear strike happens. Yet even in your new incarnation as a few handfuls of carbon, you'll want to be treated with proper deference and respect. Start thinking now about arranging a special gold chalice in which you can be carried around the post-apocalyptic hellscape by any survivors.

'To your impending divorce!'

SOW DISCORD

One of Putin's goals on the global game board is a 'multipolar' world. That means one that the West no longer dominates and in which blocs of countries struggle to agree coordinated actions such as sanctions.

Division in and between the US and Europe is therefore music to his ears, and is one reason why British voters are thought to have been targeted by Russian Twitter bots and paid ads in the run-up to the Brexit vote.

Be More Vlad

If you're feeling outnumbered and marginalised by an EU-style love-in, it's time to act.

Suppose your housemates keep ganging up on you about spending too much time in the shower. Create discord by binge-eating all Chris's expensive cheeses and leaving the wrappers scattered around Kirsten's room, then stick Sam's new red dress in Chloé's white wash.

Soon you'll be on your way to a multipolar household in which conflict is the norm and hour-long showers go unpunished.

'Maybe now you'll tell me what LOL and BRB mean?'

BLOCK PRIVATE COMMUNICATIONS

As a former intelligence officer, Putin knows the importance of private communications, and the even greater importance of banning them.

When popular Russian messaging app Telegram refused to give up the encryption keys that would let agents snoop on conversations, the Russian censor launched a crackdown. They started blocking IP addresses associated with the app, an effort that caused extra anger when it took down parts of Google as well.

Be More Vlad

If you've got foreign friends who speak to each other in a language you don't understand, you'll know how Putin felt. For all you know they could be planning terrorist acts or making fun of your hair.

Keep the world and your dignity safe by vociferously insisting that only your native language is spoken in your earshot, wherever in the world you go.

'Why would I eat this cake when I can make my own at home?'

DESTROY FOOD YOU DON'T LIKE

Huge cheese wheels crushed by bulldozers. Thirty-five tonnes of pork sent up in flames. Crates of fresh peaches dumped from the back of a lorry.

Putin's counter-sanctions policy has led to some bizarre scenes, with importers ordered to video themselves destroying perfectly good food. The images did not go down well in a country with a painful history of famine, but state media claims the hardline measures have helped boost business for home-grown producers.

Be More Vlad

You too can retaliate against your neighbours by destroying their food. Next time they ask you over, simply dump a plate of their vols-au-vent onto the carpet and grind them under your heel. They'll soon get the message about their yappy little dog.

'Your desk belongs to me now.'

ANNEX TERRITORY

In February 2014, soldiers with no insignia swarmed over the Russian-Ukrainian border into Crimea.

These 'little green men',[32] acknowledged later to be Russian special forces, seized government buildings, the parliament and the airport. Despite protests from the international community, Crimea was soon under Russian control and Putin was toasting the return of 'krym nash' – 'our Crimea!'.

Be More Vlad

You can expand your borders just as easily. If you live in an apartment block, for example, why not quietly 'occupy' the communal spaces and declare to your neighbours that they're part of your ancestral homeland?

You probably don't have any tanks to deploy, but moving your sofa into the foyer and pinning up family portraits in the hallways will send a clear message that the building is now your personal tsardom. True, you'll be making a bet that no one will do much to stop you, but so did Putin and it seems to have worked out fine for him.

'Give me a quick summary of what happened in the first two hours.'

BE DELIBERATELY LATE

Putin's lateness is legendary. The Kremlin is usually full of foreign leaders, dignitaries and bereaved parents whom he's kept waiting. His ex-wife Lyudmila's abiding memory of their first dates is sitting by herself crying because Vlad was late again. Even God has to take his turn: Putin was a full hour late for a key summit with the Pope.

Be More Vlad

Assuming this is a calculated strategy to put others off-balance, it's one you can easily apply in your own life. Whether you're heading to the theatre, catching a flight, or stepping out to see a solar eclipse, be like Putin and dilly-dally for a couple of hours first. You won't miss much except for when you do, and it's your way of showing the universe you don't dance to anyone's schedule but your own.

'I love your necklace. It would look great on me!'

IF YOU LIKE IT, TAKE IT

Putin is said to have a klepto streak as wide as the River Volga.

When Robert Kraft, owner of the New England Patriots American football club, showed him his 124-diamond-encrusted Superbowl ring, Putin asked for a closer look – and that was the last Kraft saw of his blinging trophy. 'He put it in his pocket, and three KGB guys got around him and walked out.'[33]

At the White House's urging, Kraft did the diplomatic thing and pretended it had been a gift, but he couldn't keep the secret forever and a few years later admitted what had really happened.

Be More Vlad

Why shouldn't you have all the sparkly things too? Suppose you're meeting your daughter's partner for the first time and their slick-looking diver's watch catches your eye. Ask if you can take a look, then absent-mindedly strap the watch onto your wrist and change the subject. Most likely it'll be too awkward for them to ask for it back (and if they do, you can tell your daughter they made a racist remark).

FROM THE KREMLIN
TO YOUR CUBICLE

'Jeff, I'm putting you in charge as long as you do exactly as I say.'

FIND A STOOGE

It's easy to forget that from 2008 to 2012 Putin was not president. That's because, after he hit Russia's two-term limit, he picked Dmitry Medvedev as his successor – who promptly appointed Putin in turn as prime minister.

For a while people wondered if genuine change was afoot. But it soon became clear that Putin's power base and Medvedev's junior status made the job swap pretty much meaningless. And in 2012 Vlad smoothly resumed his position, this time with an extended term limit (which he'd quietly introduced during the so-called tandem years).

Be More Vlad

A Medvedev equivalent could work wonders for your career too. Just recruit a pliant weak-chinned stooge straight from business school, elevate them swiftly above their station and pull their strings with a series of hollow promises and meaningless job-title upgrades until it's time to push them onto their sword, pin all your most dreadful decisions on them and promote them at last to Global Chief Executive Scapegoat.

Bye bye, stooge, your work here is done.

'This is where we keep the HR dossier on Alan.'

KNOW WHERE THE SKELETONS ARE

Business secrets are said to be one of the main sources of Putin's supremacy.

As head of the FSB, he apparently made it his business to collect detailed files on bribes, tax dodges, dummy companies and secret assets. Rather than use all this info to destroy his oligarch rivals, he is said to have let them continue with the threat of what he knew hanging over their heads. It meant he had pet billionaires to lean on for all his financing needs – and if they dared meddle in politics, they'd find their shady dealings dragged up in court.

Be More Vlad

If you have access to secrets on your colleagues, you're in a good position for a spot of light extortion. If not, you may need to go on a fishing expedition. Leave notes on everyone's desk reading, 'I know what you did. Meet me in the server room at 4 p.m.' Hopefully at least someone will bite and you can use your newfound informational leverage to wangle a better parking space, or one of those swanky office chairs with the seat that looks like a tongue.

'We had some brilliant candidates but I've decided to go with
my best mate from school, Jonno. God knows he's gone through a
hard patch lately and if anyone deserves a break, he does.'

LOOK AFTER OLD FRIENDS

St Petersburg, 1968: a couple of twelve-year-olds practise martial arts moves on each other at the local sambo club.

Fast-forward fifty years: one of them now runs Russia and has hoisted the other up to be one of the country's wealthiest businessmen and state contractors.

Putin's apparent trust issues seem to have resulted in him awarding lucrative projects and government jobs to old friends, bodyguards and judo-sparring partners like Arkady Rotenberg.

They might not do the greatest job in the world but loyalty is assured.

Be More Vlad

If you're involved in hiring for your company, make a list of all the qualifications the successful candidate will need, then throw it away and follow Putin's example by hiring Sam, that girl you used to go trampolining with when you were kids. Having her around will remind you of simpler times, plus you've heard she's in a really bad place so if you get her the job she'll be permanently in your debt. The ideal combination.

'You must be from the agency? Right, the plan is we go into the office,
I parade you all round a bit and then you're free to go.'

SHOW YOUR FAMILY VALUES

One of Putin's KGB colleagues believed he married for his career, bachelorhood being seen as a bit suspicious in 1980s USSR. If so, it seems to have worked, as Putin's big promotion followed hot on his wedding day.

Years later, on Valentine's Day 2008, a corny romantic movie appeared that tried to burnish Putin's image as a husband. *A Kiss off the Record* centred on a romance between a politician obviously modelled on Putin and a woman obviously modelled on Lyudmila. Yet real-life appearances of the Putins were visibly strained, and soon afterwards they split up.

Be More Vlad

If you have traditionally minded superiors, you'll want to create the illusion that you're a family man or woman. The good news is there's no need to spend time with your actual family. Instead, hire a professional photographer to snap you and some stand-ins having fun in front of a green screen. With just a few hours' Photoshopping, you'll have enough images to show your bosses a different day out every time they ask, leaving you free to focus on what really matters: the single-minded pursuit of power.

'Morning, everyone, I thought it was time you all
got a look at my fantastic navel.'

SHOW OFF YOUR BEST FEATURE

An estimated forty-eight inches in circumference, Putin's chest is widely regarded as a Eurasian marvel. To not get it out periodically, as Putin has done while riding a horse, pole fishing, swimming butterfly stroke and so on, would be unfair to both Russia and the world.

The famous chest isn't just a side of prime ribs either; it tells the people that Putin is a man of vigour and iron will, a world away from the flab and drunkenness of his predecessor, Boris Yeltsin.

'How can one not vote for such a torso?' Moscow tabloid *MK* asked,[34] somewhat sardonically.

Be More Vlad

If there's a feature you're especially proud of, get it out for your workmates to see – whether it's a broad upper back that suggests you're ready to take on new responsibilities; toned calves that promise you're in it for the long run; or a shapely set of kneecaps that somehow bespeak proficiency in Microsoft Office.

'I'll have my usual tea, Sandra, and could you put it in my manager's goblet?'

DISPLAY YOUR STATUS

'Ponty' is slang for Russia's elaborate system of status symbols and there's no better example than Moscow's 'special highway'.

The eight-lane route links the Kremlin with Putin's residence in the woods. But instead of a central reservation, there is a ninth lane that only a tiny number of ultra-privileged Muscovites can use.

The median lane is of such fascination that local status-watchers note down every vehicle and VIP using it. Of course, traffic is only shut off completely for Putin himself, as well as for his prime minister Dmitry Medvedev, which must make them both feel pretty special.

Be More Vlad

If your company culture runs on ponty, consider having your colleagues carry you around in a sedan chair with a personalised number plate. You could even get them to carry you to the posh supermarket to stock up on organic crackers and those ready meals that come in a sort of basket.

You are extra special, and deserve never to be confronted with the terrifying thought that you might not be.

*'28 . . . 29 . . . 30. And that's why you should
give me a job building spreadsheets.'*

HIT THE GYM

Of all Putin's strengths as a leader, his strength may be the strongest of all.

Even in his sixties, he takes working out as seriously as his grip on power, lifting weights with his political comrades in a Loro Piana tracksuit retailing for $3,200, then swimming for two hours every single day. How reassuring for the Russian people to know that their leader could whup Donald Trump in a brawl, as well as geopolitically.

Be More Vlad

If you want to win trust in your workplace it's well worth developing a fighting physique like Vlad's. It lets your colleagues know that even in the event of a second Cold War and ensuing apocalypse, you have the brute strength to defend them from marauding gangs, gather fuel and drag infected bodies to be incinerated, with energy left over to prepare for that big Q2 sales conference.

'Hannah from Finance doesn't wash her hands, and that's not all I could tell you.'

GATHER 'KOMPROMAT' ON YOUR ENEMIES

Putin and his people are known as apparent masters of incriminating material, like the video of Russia's prosecutor general with two prostitutes that helped clear the way for Putin's rapid ascent in the nineties.

Be More Vlad

You can do something similar to get ahead at your workplace. Try baking a lovely chocolate cake and bringing it in to your office. Notice which of your colleagues take two slices, and who's left with none, then draw a sketch of what happened on a Post-it note.

You've just created strategic leverage over the greedy co-worker – and the chance to instil a grudge in the hungry one.

With power moves of this calibre, you'll soon be one of the most formidable figures in regional sales.

'You're welcome and since I've held the door for you a few times now, I was
wondering if you might help me repaint my bathroom this weekend?'

ACCUMULATE 'BLAT'

'Blat' is the informal network of favours and connections among Soviet elites, and Putin was a master at it. He got his first big Moscow job through blat, thanks to two contacts he'd schmoozed in the halls of St Petersburg.[35]

Blat remains a vital currency in today's Russia if you want to get things done. Fortunately, Putin can top up his blat current account by handing out valuable contracts. It's a case of 'I scratch your back; you give me rights to build parallel bridges over the Kerch Strait.'

Be More Vlad

If you'd like to grow a power base in your little corner of the world, you'll need to accumulate some blat of your own. That means making sure the favours you do are remembered. Why not create readymade blat cards to hand out to people, with messages such as: '[Insert name here] just offered you a biscuit', 'Remember that time [Insert name here] lent you her umbrella?' or '[Insert name here] fed your goldfish that time. What will you do for [Insert name here]?'.

'Insects! Bow down before your new assistant floor manager!'

SHOW PEOPLE WHO'S IN CHARGE

When a factory closed in Pikalevo in 2009, townspeople were left unwaged and angry. They blocked highways, occupied the mayor's office and went on hunger strike.

To stop the spreading chaos, Putin travelled to the little town to give the managers responsible a bollocking for the ages. With cameras looking on, he compared them to cockroaches.

'Give me back my pen,'[36] he snarled, after making the chief cockroach sign a statement of culpability.

By the time he'd finished, millions in back wages had flowed into workers' bank accounts and Vlad had proved that he alone could fix the people's problems.

Be More Vlad

If you find your household in disarray during the summer holidays, wrest back control of the situation Putin-style by shouting at the cat so eloquently and forcefully that the other members of your family have to sit up and take notice. The cat won't really mind and everyone else will finally comprehend that it's *really* not a good idea to mess with you right now.

'You do realise couscous was invented by Mossad?'

LOOK OUT FOR CONSPIRACIES

Putin seemingly sees enemy spooks everywhere, believing their influence and money bags are the hidden reason behind everything that goes wrong for him.

Evidence of possible paranoid tendencies includes his apparent belief that the internet is a CIA project that Russians need to be protected from,[37] and the recent expansion of his food and drink tasting team in case of poisoning attempts.[38]

Neurotic maybe, but from a man who's survived peak CIA/KGB skulduggery in the Cold War, as well as multiple assassination attempts, not exactly surprising.

Be More Vlad

Though you may have less reason to fear hidden forces than Putin, a touch of paranoia could be your friend. After all, being overly relaxed about outlandish possibilities never saved anyone from being attacked by the lizard people who live inside the walls.

'He's a truly terrible accountant but you have to give him points for style.'

BE A WILD CHILD

Putin is seldom upstaged, so when new president Barack Obama visited Moscow to global fanfare in 2009, he went into full-on attention-seeking mode.

Dressed in black, Putin rode out before the crowds on a Harley Davidson trike, closely followed by his pals the Night Wolves, an 11,000-strong nationalist motorcycle gang led by a very nice man called 'the Surgeon'.[39]

Images of Bad Vlad leading the gang got almost as much coverage as Obama's big speech the same week. Mission accomplished?

Be More Vlad

When your oh-so-perfect sister comes home for Christmas, all glowing from her volunteer medical work in Africa, you know you can't out-virtue her. So steal her limelight Putin-style instead. You could dress in fishnets and invite some random guys from the scrapyard to join your family's Christmas dinner. Tell your parents they're your 'husbands for the holidays' and the way they smell makes you feel like an animal in the best way.

Let's face it, your mum and dad will never love you the best, but at least showing your wild side will get you some of their attention.

ADVANCED
REPUTATION HACKING

'MUM! Dad's sellotaped a picture of his face to the TV again.'

DOMINATE THE MEDIA

The Vladimir Putin Show has such a hold on Russian media that it's hard for anyone else to get a look in.

Quickly after he became president, Putin had security forces raid independent station NTV.[40] Papers were removed, debts called in, and pretty soon NTV had been taken over by a state-owned conglomerate.

Today, most of the big channels are state-controlled, including Channel One, Russia One and RT.[41] Few independent news agencies can scratch a living and even fewer will challenge the core tenets of Putin's political system.

Be More Vlad

It might seem unthinkable that you could dominate people's media consumption to the degree Putin does, but with today's social media, it's possible. Start uploading videos of yourself striking power poses, intercut with stock footage of worshipful crowds. Repeat this incessantly enough and you can drown out the kitten and baby photos and trap your friends in a hall of mirrors with you and your glorious opinions around every corner.

Soon your propaganda will take hold and you'll have an adoring online army at your command (at least, if they don't all block you first).

'Babe, you did it, congratulations! Listen, any idea when
the free bar ends tonight? I need to book a taxi.'

KNOW WHEN TO LEAVE A PARTY

One of Putin's canny decisions was to quit the KGB and distance himself from the Communist Party at just the moment the Soviet collapse became inevitable. His well-timed leap, on 20 August 1991, landed him on the right side of history without him appearing like too much of a revolutionary (important at a time when most Russians craved stability).

Be More Vlad

Timing your exit from a big party could be equally crucial. You want to be there for the best nibbles, Instagrammable moments and at least the first bit of dancing. But you want to leave before it all falls apart, Soviet-style. If the other guests begin a heated discussion about which bit of your anatomy would be best for doing cocaine out of, for example, it's time to get out of there.

'Neighbour, it was me who keyed your car. I've been feeling
awful about it but now I've told you we can all move on.'

CONFESS BEFORE YOU'RE FOUND OUT

In the early nineties, Putin's secret KGB past had become a liability. A link to the loathed organisation was a blackmail risk in the new Russia and could have seriously damaged Vlad's career as an up-and-coming political aide.

So he decided to defuse the ticking time bomb by orchestrating a confession on TV. Carefully rehearsed and helped by a heroic soundtrack, he came clean on his own terms and managed to make himself sound less like a hated internal repressor and more like an international man of mystery.

Be More Vlad

If you're living with a secret that's bound to come out, limit the damage and confess as Vlad did. You probably won't be able to arrange a TV interview, so write your secret on a T-shirt and dance around in the background of a live news report instead. It'll feel good to get your secret off your chest, and who knows, maybe your main family and secret family will get along just fine.

'Sorry to leave the party early, guys.
I have to take this injured bee to the vet.'

SHOW YOUR GENTLE SIDE

To win respect you must be ruthless. To win love you need to show a softer side. Putin's approach is to help his country's cutest animals at every opportunity.

He's been photographed feeding a baby elk outside Moscow; rehabilitating cranes in Siberia; releasing rescued tigers back into the wild in Amur Oblast; and shaking hands with a walrus in Vladivostok.

Be More Vlad

If you're known as a workplace meanie, show your colleagues you're actually quite nice by booking a day off and hiring a professional photographer to join you on a trip to the petting zoo. Then share the photos far and wide with plenty of squidgy emoticons. Be sure to wait at least twenty minutes before returning to your hardass persona.

(Note that while at the zoo you may wish to avoid Putin's other habit of kissing small children's bellies. Some things only presidents get away with.)

*'I love a giggle as much as the next person, but anyone who
laughs at my new hat is fired with immediate effect.'*

STAMP OUT MOCKERY

Putin knows that jokes can be a serious threat to his power and he'll go to great lengths to stop them.

In 2000 his team is said to have quickly had an unflattering puppet of him removed from the satirical TV programme *Kukly*.[42] More recently an infamous meme of him with rouged lips and painted eyelashes was on a list of 4,074 banned 'extremist materials'.[43]

Since the list was made public, the 'Putin gay clown' image (extremist item number 4,071) has been viewed millions of times, despite concerned internet users around the world tweeting the image with clear instructions not to share. We can only imagine how much worse things would have been if the Kremlin had taken a less firm line.

Be More Vlad

If you're fed up of jokes at your expense, follow Putin's strategy and make a list. If you're a teacher, write out all the unacceptable nicknames your pupils call you and stick them up on giant posters around the school. This way, the troublemakers will know exactly what they're not allowed to say and you can reclaim the respect and courtesy to which you're entitled.

'Lisa was a wonderful woman who, just before she died,
confessed she had been online gambling using my identity.'

BLAME THE DEAD

Another ploy Putin has used is to find someone to blame who can't respond (at least in this world).

Anti-corruption lawyer Sergei Magnitsky collected evidence that law enforcement officials had stolen $230m in tax money. But instead of investigating, the authorities levelled the fraud charges at Magnitsky himself.

At the time of his jailing he was a healthy thirty-six-year-old. A year later, he was discovered dead in his cell, plagued with untreated medical problems and bruised from beatings.

Charges were brought against him anyway – the first time a deceased person has been put on trial in Russian history.[44]

Be More Vlad

Although people who've moved on from your workplace are not strictly speaking dead, pinning blame on them is a useful way to draw a line under a problem. Wasn't it Sandra, who used to work in the canteen, for example, who embezzled all that training money and stank up the men's toilets? Yes, it was definitely her. Until Ajay from Operations leaves and then it'll be his fault.

'Young lady, I've garnered opinion and everyone agrees that your piercings are disgusting.'

STAND WITH THE MORAL MAJORITY

Who will speak for all the right-thinking citizens out there? Putin does, and you can too.

Punk band Pussy Riot are among the best-known resisters in Russia thanks to their mediagenic protest art. In 2013 they were imprisoned for 'hooliganism motivated by religious hatred' after singing an anti-Putin song called 'Holy Shit' in a Moscow cathedral. Their treatment was heavily criticised in the West but many Russians thought they got what they deserved, regarding the performance as an affront to the Church.

Grasping this, Putin weighed in strongly, saying 'They got what they asked for . . . One must not erode our moral foundation and undermine the country'.[45]

Be More Vlad

You too can take a courageous stance on a current issue based on what others think. For example, next time someone makes a joke about a recent tragedy (dead musician, terror attack, cancellation of TV show), ask yourself: was that 'too soon'? Read the room – if you see pursed lips or shaking heads, now's the time to speak up, flounce out and score some brownie points with the moral majority.

'Okay, guys, I want you all to forget about next week's lay-offs –
today is about fun!'

HOLD A SPORTS DAY

Ever since the boycotted 1980 Moscow Olympics, the Russian people have been waiting for a great leader to bring back the Games and restore Russia to its rightful place atop the international rostrum.

The Sochi 2014 Winter Games were Putin's chance. He flung money at them to ensure success, in the end splashing out $51 billion.[46] That's more than any Olympics in history and five times more than the 2018 World Cup, but worth it to show everyone what Russia is capable of.

Be More Vlad

If you feel your neighbours aren't giving you the respect and admiration you're due, invite them all to a no-expense-spared sports day in your street.

Yes, it will be a mad race to get everything ready. Yes, you'll have to max out your credit cards to bribe the woman from the council to let you close the street. Yes, the portaloos will overflow and your housemates won't be happy when you present them with an enormous surprise bill for their share of the cost. Yes, yes, yes.

But it'll all be worth it when those hypocrites across the road have to admit you put on the best welly wang ever.

'I do . . . Or do I?'

'I do . . . Or do I?'

BE AN ENIGMA

Since Putin's divorce he's courted intrigue by being extravagantly coy about his relationship status.

He has denied rumours of a fling with a gymnast, but in 2014 told journalists: 'A friend of mine from Europe, a big boss, recently asked me, after what happened last year: "Listen, is there a love in your life?"

'I say, "In what sense?"

'"Do you love anyone?"

'I say, "Yes."

'"And does anyone love you?"

'I say, "Yes."

'He must have decided that I had completely gone wild.

'"Thank God," he said, before downing the vodka. "Everything is fine. Do not worry."'[47]

Be More Vlad

To make yourself as romantic and mysterious as Vlad, try varying the way you say goodbye. By constantly switching between passionate tonguings and stiff, formal handshakes, you can keep everyone guessing about the tempestuous nature of your relationships, leaving you free to get on with quietly expanding your zone of influence.

'By the way I just found some Bronze Age earthenware under your sofa.'

CASUALLY FIND AN ANCIENT RELIC

On only his third scuba dive, Putin was filmed discovering a haul of ancient Greek amphoras just two metres below the calm, clear surface of the Black Sea.

'Treasure!' he told reporters with a grin.[48]

Despite the popularity of the diving spot, the priceless pottery must have gone unnoticed for over 1,400 years. Incredible!

Be More Vlad

Why not conveniently stumble upon a historically important relic of your own and show your friends how keen-eyed and cosmically lucky you are?

If stuck for rare artefacts to plant, simply bury some gold pieces (aka chocolate coins) at the park, and get a passer-by to film you excitedly digging them up.

'I hope you don't mind, I'm just making a few edits to your diary.'

REWRITE HISTORY

Putin's Russia runs on national pride. So it's no surprise he's made some tweaks to some of the nation's less glorious chapters.

A textbook for history teachers that Putin put his weight behind[49] seemed to excuse Stalin – generally regarded as one of history's great monsters – for merely doing what the circumstances of World War Two demanded. Meanwhile the Perm-36 Gulag Museum in Siberia has been taken over by the state and relaunched to celebrate the camp's role in beating the Nazis, ignoring the brutal labour forced on dissidents there.[50]

Be More Vlad

You too can rewrite the embarrassing parts of your history. Say you've been looking at some websites you'd rather your family didn't know about (perhaps you've been doing research for an academic paper on human desire, which you'd naturally like to be a surprise). With a little savvy, you can erase your browsing history with a trail to something more savoury, like a page on how to knit sweaters for orphaned wallabies – innocent in the knowledge that you're merely indulging in some mild Putinesque revisionism.

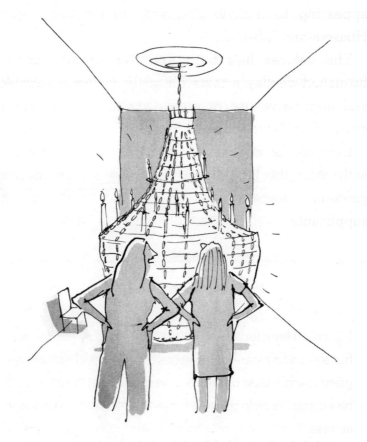

'We were going to go for the bare lightbulb look but we thought fuck it.'

SAY NO TO UNDERSTATEMENT

Putin wields interior design like a weapon, with influences appearing to include Emperor Nicholas II, Saddam Hussein and Liberace.

The palaces he's built and the aircraft he's had furnished display a taste for scale, baroque splendour and aggressive use of gold ormolu, with all subtlety crushed under tonnage of marble.

Even his secret pleasure residence at Cape Idokopas – with casino, theatre, helipads, lavish frescoes and courtyard gardens – seems calculated to dwarf and intimidate supplicants.

Be More Vlad

It's a hard look for the rest of us to pull off on a shoestring, but even a few statement pieces (jewel-encrusted loo seat, giant marble bust of yourself next to the dishwasher) can be enough to help prevent your visitors ever feeling truly at ease.

'Keep up at the back, scooter section! I want a tight
formation as we pass Auntie Pam's house!'

STAGE A PARADE

Holding a parade is a cheerful, fun and inclusive way to show people how much death you can dish out.

In 2008 Putin revived the Soviet tradition of military parades through Red Square. The stated goal was to remember the eightieth anniversary of the Great Patriotic War (that's Russian for World War Two), but the vehicles on display weren't from the forties. They included an array of powerful new tanks and mobile missile systems capable of launching long-range nuclear strikes – a testament to Putin's increased military spending.

Be More Vlad

If you would like to use the firepower at your disposal to impress your sweetheart or intimidate a rival, consider putting on a parade in the park where they have lunch. Technically speaking, only three vehicles are required to constitute a parade, so you could stage one with as few troops as one car, one bike and a Roomba robot vacuum. If you really want to shock and awe your audience, why not throw in a ground-to-air missile launcher as well (aka a young relative carrying a catapult)?

AFTERWORD

Once you've tried all the tips in this book, many of the problems you may have in life will melt away. That's the *Vladimir Putin: Life Coach* Promise™.

However, now that you are the reigning figure in your street or office pod, a new problem may rear its head: the fear that your newfound supremacy could one day end. That someone even more cunning could come along and overthrow you (e.g. kick you off the allotment committee and take your parking spot).

We do not know if Putin himself has such worries. Maybe, once in a long while, when he's swimming meditative lengths of the Kremlin pool, a whisper of self-doubt reaches him from a distant wing of his mind palace, warning him that his luck can't last forever.

If so, he hasn't let on. Nor has he revealed any clever techniques for dealing with such worries. So we are sadly unable to offer a final Putin-inspired tip for advanced students anxious about maintaining their grip on power.

Instead, we recommend you seek further advice from

the man himself, via his annual phone-in show, *Direct Line with Vladimir Putin,* broadcast on live TV by Russia 1, Russia 24, RT and Channel One Russia.

Удачи, товарищи

ENDNOTES

1 'Russia tested nerve agent on door handes before Skripal attack, UK dossier claims' *Guardian*, 13th April, 2018

2 From *Vladimir Putin: The Road to Power* by Oleg Blotsky, cited in article 'Book Details the Unenviable Life of Mrs Vladimir V. Putin', *LA Times*, 16th September, 2002

3 'Putin's lakeside "notables" targeted in sanctions', *Reuters*, 21st March, 2014

4 'Silvio Berlusconi and Vladimir Putin are on the bed together', *The Times*, 9 October, 2017

5 'St Petersburg "troll farm" had 90 dedicated staff working to influence US election campaign', *Independent*, 17th October, 2017

6 'Inside the Russian Troll Factory: Zombies and a Breakneck Pace', *New York Times*, 18th February, 2018

7 Rice, Condoleeza (2011), *No Greater Honour*, Crown Publishing, Penguin Random House

8 'Bush's Love of Pootie-Poot Putin', *Guardian*, 20th May, 2002

9 'Russian Observers Charge Fraud in Putin's Landslide Re-Election', Bloomberg.com, 19th March, 2018

10 'Ballot stuffing, vote-rigging and fraud: Russians on alert for tricks that may help Vladimir Putin win election', *Telegraph*, 12th February 2012

11 'The Trumps of Russia?' *Guardian*, 15th July, 2017

12 'Why Does Vladimir Putin Keep Giving His Watches Away to Peasants?' *Vice*, 17th September, 2013

13 'Former aide says Putin has no strategic plans', *Time*, 5th November 2014

14 Zygar, Mikhail (2016), *All the Kremlin's Men*, Public Affairs, Perseus Books Group

15 'Putin tells Edward Snowden: Russia doesn't carry out mass surveillance', *Guardian*, 17ᵗʰ April, 2014

16 'Vladimir Putin presents Steven Seagal with Russian passport', *Guardian*, 25ᵗʰ November, 2016

17 Myers, Steven Lee (2015), *The New Tsar: The Rise and Reign of Vladimir Putin*, Alfred A. Knopf

18 'Revealed: the $2bn offshore trail that leads to Vladimir Putin', *Guardian*, 3ʳᵈ April, 2016

19 'Panama Papers: Who is Sergei Roldugin', *International Business Times*, 4ᵗʰ April, 2016

20 'No one knows Putin's exact net worth, but many speculate he's the wealthiest person on the planet', *Business Insider*, 17ᵗʰ March, 2018

21 'Cut-and-paste job: "My father wrote Putin's dissertation"', RFE/RL, 7ᵗʰ March, 2018

22 'Russia's plagiarism problem: even Putin has done it!' *Washington Post*, 18ᵗʰ March, 2014

23 Kasparov, Garry (2015), *Winter is Coming*, Public Affairs, Perseus Books Group

24 'What about that "whataboutism"', *San Francisco Chronicle*, 10ᵗʰ September, 2017

25 Hillary Clinton on the *Late Show with Stephen Colbert*, 19ᵗʰ September, 2017

26 'The Aussie who taught Putin Body Language', *Moscow Times*, 1ˢᵗ July, 2018

27 'In Sochi, the mark of a Russian vodka oligarch', *The New Yorker*, 20ᵗʰ February, 2014

28 'Here are ten critics of Vladimir Putin who died violently or in suspicious ways', *Washington Post*, 23ʳᵈ March, 2017

29 'Putin on Isis', *Financial Times*, 23ʳᵈ October, 2015

30 'Berezovsky quits Duma, at "ruining of Russia"', *Independent*, 18th July, 2000

31 'Putin, before vote, unveils "invincible" nuclear weapons to counter West', Reuters, 1st March, 2018

32 'Putin Comes Clean on Crimea's Little Green Men', *Sky News*, 10th March, 2015

33 'How Vladimir Putin Rose to Power', *Business Insider*, 14th February, 2017

34 'Рыболовный анонс предвыборной кампании: зачем оголился Путин', *MKRU*, 6th August, 2017

35 Myers, Steven Lee (2015), *The New Tsar: The Rise and Reign of Vladimir Putin*, Alfred A. Knopf

36 'Putin erupts in struggling Russian town', *CBS News*, 8th June, 2009

37 'Putin calls internet "a CIA project"', *Guardian*, 24th April, 2014

38 '"Paranoid" Vladimir Putin hires even more food and drink tasters', *Mirror*, 11th March, 2018

39 'Analysis: Sidelined Vladimir Putin turns to motorcycle tricks', *Telegraph*, 8th July, 2009

40 'Russian Network Seized in Raid', *Washington Post*, 15th April, 2001

41 'Country Profile: Russia', *BBC News*, 6th March, 2012

42 'Satire is thriving in Russia, while many Russians aren't', *Newsweek*, 2nd May, 2016

43 'It's now illegal in Russia to share an image of Putin as a gay clown', *Washington Post*, 5th April, 2017

44 'Russia puts Sergei Magnitsky on trial – three years after he died in custody', *Guardian*, 8th March, 2015

45 'Putin says Pussy Riot "got what they asked for" as jailed women appeal', *Guardian*, 8th October, 2012

46 'Sochi: the costliest Olympics yet', *Guardian*, 9th October, 2013

47 'Russian President Vladimir Putin "in love" with gymnast Alina Kabayeva, *Express*, 20th December, 2014

48 'Putin "finds" Greek urn on dive, news.com.au, 11th August, 2011

49 'The Rewriting of History', *Economist*, 8th November, 2007

50 'The Kremlin is trying to erase memories of the Gulag', *New Republic*, 23rd June, 2014

ACKNOWLEDGEMENTS

With special thanks to Hannah Knowles, Gordon Wise, Jamie Byng, John Sears, Belinda Sears and Grace McGeoch.